*How precious is Your love,
O God! We take refuge in the
shadow of Your wings.
Psalm 36:8*

The intent and
purpose of this volume is to
give you faith, hope and
inspiration. Hopefully it will help bring
peace and tranquility into your life. May
it be a reminder of God's love, guidance
and His many blessings.

Our publications help to support our work
for needy children in over 130 countries
around the world. Through our
programs, thousands of children are
fed, clothed, educated, sheltered
and given the opportunity to
live decent lives.

Salesian Missions wishes to extend special thanks and gratitude to our generous poet friends and to the publishers who have given us permission to reprint material included in this book. Every effort has been made to give proper acknowledgments. Any omissions or errors are deeply regretted, and the publisher, upon notification, will be pleased to make the necessary corrections in subsequent editions.

Cover photo: ©Corbis/artzooks.com

First Edition Printed in the U.S.A. by Concord Litho Group, Concord, NH 03301.

Expressions of His Love
from the
Salesian Collection

Compiled and Edited
by Jennifer Grimaldi

Illustrated by
Russell Bushée, Paul Scully, Frank Massa,
Helen M.L. Kunic, Bob Pantelone,
Terrie Meider, Maureen McCarthy,
and Robert VanSteinburg

Contents

A New Day

A whole new day confronts me now
With challenges to meet.
I will go forth with confidence
Without delusion or defeat.
My Lord is here beside me
As I strive to forge ahead
With utmost optimism
On the pathways where I tread.
I will not let adversity
Allow my faith to quell;
I'll lean upon my Lord this day
Trusting… all goes well.
This whole new day holds promises
I will conquer and achieve.
I cannot fail nor foster fear
When I continue to believe.

I know that yesterday is gone –
Not to dwell on failures past;
I'll make the most of every hour
As long as this day will last.
I will take pride in all I do,
My values are redefined;
This day will be exemplified,
For God controls my heart and mind.
A whole new day He gives to me,
Fresh and new and free from sins.
My life restored… God's love prevails…
I smile as this new day begins.

Patience Allison Hartbauer

Spring Is in the Air

Do you hear the little, green peepers
Piping all night long?
Do you hear the wind in the treetops
Singing a different song?
The earth is awakening from slumber;
There's excitement in the air.
Warm is the kiss of sunshine,
Beckoning flowers so fair.
Birds have returned to the meadows;
Their song is a constant delight.
Soft shades of green robe the hillsides,
How welcome this beautiful sight.
Enchanting is the Spring season,
Every heart has a melody.
Broken is Winter's bondage,
Our spirits are merry and free.

Regina Wiencek

His Marvelous Light

If you have felt a gentle breeze
Brush lightly on your cheek,
Or heard the rippling water
Flowing gently down the creek…
Or seen a little wren, so small,
Fly blithely through the sky,
Or smelled a flower's succulent scent,
Or heard a baby cry…
Then you have had great privilege –
Through hearing and through sight,
You smelled the sweet aroma
And saw His marvelous light;
You have heard the voice of God,
You've seen His love and grace;
For this His handiwork is spread –
Just look most anyplace.
And you have seen the Savior, too,
As sure as if He's been
Close by your side, if you have had
A heartfelt sense of Him.

Bonnie Nelson

*Rise up in splendor! Your
light has come, the glory of
the Lord shines upon you.*
Isaiah 60:1

An April Morning

On a beautiful April morning
As I was walking down the street,
I could hear the birds singing,
Their melodies so sweet.

I could see the blue sky up above
And the good, old earth beneath.
Was that God whispering to me
Or just the rustling of a leaf?

Then as it started to rain,
I began to wonder –
Was that God's voice I heard
Or just the rolling thunder?

At noon as I ate my lunch,
I thanked Him for my food,
And I had the feeling
That life was very good.

As the evening shadows lengthened,
I thought about my day;
It seemed that God was very close
All along the way.

Esther Edwards

*I trust in Your faithfulness. Grant my heart
joy in Your help, that I may sing of the Lord,
"How good our God has been to me!"*
Psalm 13:6

Just a Little Prayer

Just a little prayer, that's all,
Will ease your troubled mind,
Will touch the very heart of God –
Will help you to unwind.
Just a little prayer, that's all –
It doesn't take much time,
But when you're through you'll be amazed
How things work out just fine!

Millie Torzilli

We Thank You

We thank You for the sunshine
And we thank You for the rain.
We thank You for the gladness
And we thank You for the pain.

The sunshine makes all pleasant,
The rain makes all things grow,
The gladness keeps us happy
So that our pain won't show.

We thank You for the flowers
And blessings by the score.
We thank You for the air we breathe –
How can we ask for more?

With all these many blessings,
With life and friends to share,
Gentle Jesus, we can only ask
You keep us in Your care.

Wilma Parkin

Jesus Loves Me

Yes, Jesus loves me;
He proves this every day.
I can feel His warm embraces,
Each time I kneel to pray.

He walks with me through shadows;
He guides me where I go.
I can forge ahead with confidence,
For I live within His glow.

He lights my life with victory;
He provides everything I need.
His love gives me encouragement;
I know I can succeed.

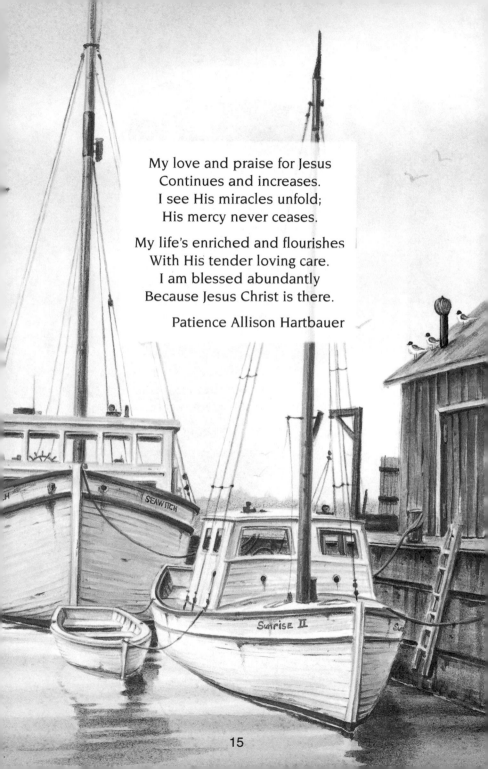

My love and praise for Jesus
Continues and increases.
I see His miracles unfold;
His mercy never ceases.

My life's enriched and flourishes
With His tender loving care.
I am blessed abundantly
Because Jesus Christ is there.

Patience Allison Hartbauer

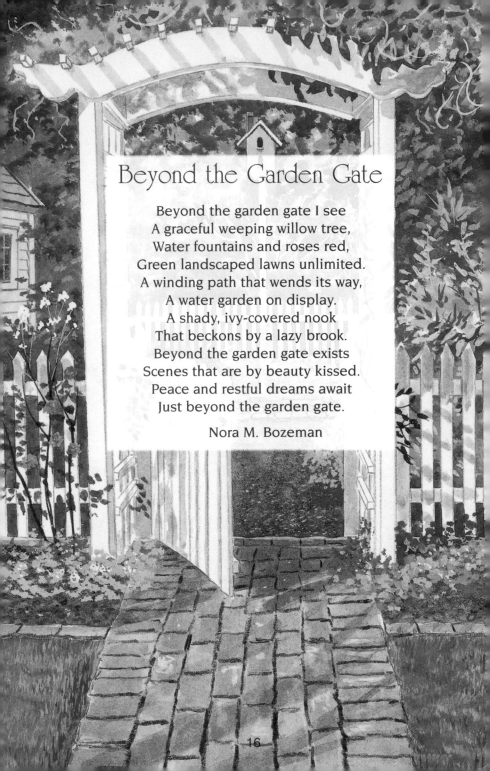

Beyond the Garden Gate

Beyond the garden gate I see
A graceful weeping willow tree,
Water fountains and roses red,
Green landscaped lawns unlimited.
A winding path that wends its way,
A water garden on display.
A shady, ivy-covered nook
That beckons by a lazy brook.
Beyond the garden gate exists
Scenes that are by beauty kissed.
Peace and restful dreams await
Just beyond the garden gate.

Nora M. Bozeman

Thankful for Each Season

I'm thankful for each season,
Whatever it may bring –
The snowflakes in the Winter
Or daffodils in Spring.

I'm thankful for the Summer sun,
The shower's soft refrain;
He who makes the sun to shine
Also sends the rain.

I'm thankful for the Autumn,
The leaves in colors bright.
I'm thankful for each pumpkin carved
That brings a child delight.

It matters not the time of year,
Skies of blue or gray;
Each season's fashioned by our God
In His own perfect way.

Kay Hoffman

*I will delight and rejoice in
You; I will sing hymns to Your
name, Most High.*
Psalm 9:3

Faith

Our lives are spent in circumspect –
We should script each page with care,
And wonder if the words we say
Are written down somewhere
To keep account lest we forget
The past things we've spoken of.
So I prefer to choose my words
By wrapping them in love.
For little words are measures of
The faith that we let grow.
Our daily satisfactions come
With the degree of it we show.

Believing isn't what we are –
It's something that we do,
Practiced whenever things go wrong
To help to get us through.
Faith is more than getting past
Those things that cause us fear;
It's also knowing in good times
That God is also near
And likes to have communion with
Each person day to day.
Faith is more than wish and want…
It's also what we say.

Nancy Watson Dodrill

My Love for You

A rose will bloom then wither,
Its petals fall away,
Unlike the love I have for you
That thrives and grows each day.
A dream lasts only seconds
And then is gone and o'er,
Unlike the love I have for you
That will last evermore.
The waves wash in upon the beach,
Sand castles wash away,
Unlike the love I have for you,
Most steadfast day by day.
The seasons come, the seasons go,
As they are bound to do,
Unlike the love within my heart
That lives each day anew.

Harold F. Mohn

His Strength and Song

He gives me strength from day to day
To face whatever comes my way;
He lifts me to great heights above
And reassures me of His love.
He walks with me when days seem long
And puts into my heart a song;
A lovely tune with sweeter words
That even stills the songs of birds…
But for a moment, then they sing
More sweeter songs the Savior brings,
Songs that lift a heavy load
When trudging down a lonesome road.
He is my hope, my joy, my life,
Who keeps me safe through storms and strife;
I'd not be able to carry on
Without His strength – without His song.

Lou Ella Cullipher

*The Lord is my strength
and my shield… with my
song I praise my God.*
Psalm 28:7

My Jesus

No matter what the future holds
Or what tomorrow brings...
I know I'm safe within the arms
Of Jesus Christ, my King.

Every day upon this earth,
I feel His spirit move...
I know He lives within my heart
To comfort and to soothe.

And when I stumble, as I will,
I'll pick myself up high...
For in my weakness, He is strong;
In darkness, He is light.

Gentle Jesus, hear me now
And dry these tears I weep.
Take the burdens that I bear
And heal me as I sleep.

And as the morning sun appears,
I'll give my thanks so true.
Another day has come again;
My Jesus, I love You.

Jill Lemming

*In green pastures You
let me graze; to safe
waters You lead me.*
Psalm 23:2

Season After Season

Season after season, our Shepherd is there,
Guiding our steps in His gentle care.
Winter and springtime, Summer and Fall,
His presence leadeth, watching over all.
Morning after morning and through every day,
He ever strengthens and shows the way.
Evening and nighttime, through the whole year,
His comfort blesses, driving away fear.
Season after season, through all our days,
Our faithful Lord, in wise, loving ways,
Cares for His children, knowing each one,
And ever leadeth 'til life's work is done.

Kathryn Thorne Bowsher

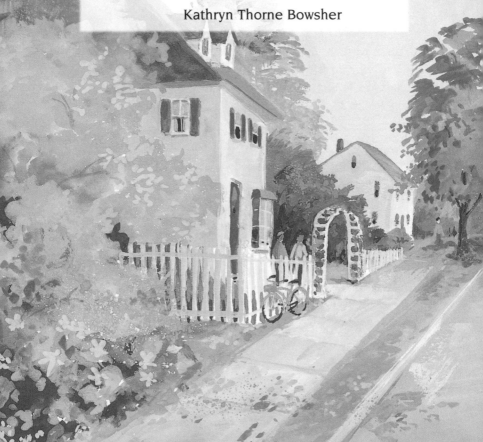

Love

Love's conversation never ends,
That inner-peace unique to friends.
It is a bond – a holy trust,
Where faith-filled couplings never rust.
It is a magic chord – a song
That feels and comforts every wrong.
It is what all God's prophets wrote,
The great composer's every note.
It is the hero's selfless deed,
Our binding pledge – our sacred Creed.
It is forever – always new,
God's living spirit shining through.
Love finds its home no matter where,
As long as you, my friend, are there.

Rich Houseknecht

*Beloved, let us love one another, because
love is of God; everyone who loves is
begotten by God and knows God.*
1 John 4:7

A Trinity of Happiness

Three things will make you happy
When they happen to you:
Someone to love, something to do and
Something to look forward to.
You will find in your friends and loved ones
A joy you've never known,
And a comfort just in knowing
That you are not alone.

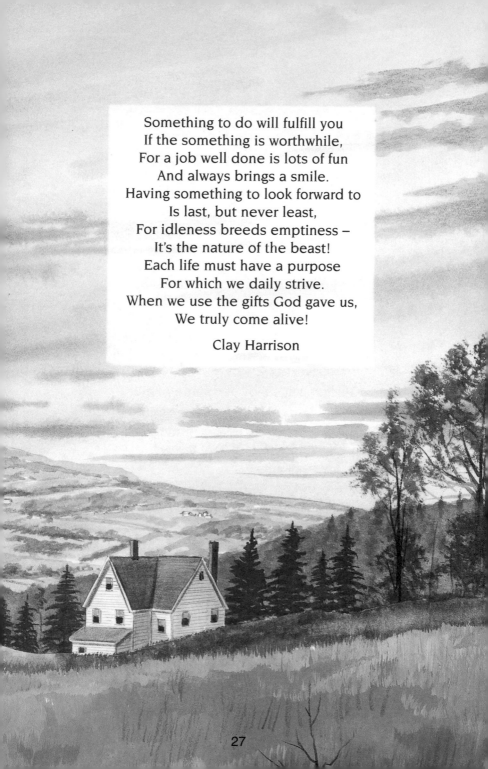

Something to do will fulfill you
If the something is worthwhile,
For a job well done is lots of fun
And always brings a smile.
Having something to look forward to
Is last, but never least,
For idleness breeds emptiness –
It's the nature of the beast!
Each life must have a purpose
For which we daily strive.
When we use the gifts God gave us,
We truly come alive!

Clay Harrison

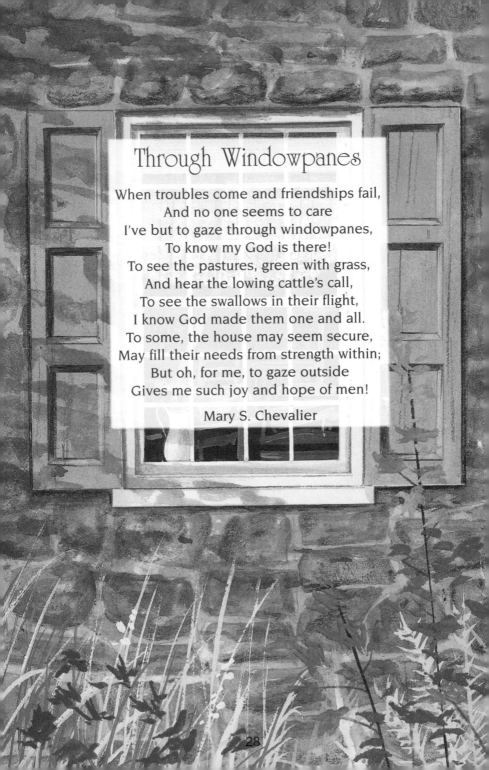

Through Windowpanes

When troubles come and friendships fail,
And no one seems to care
I've but to gaze through windowpanes,
To know my God is there!
To see the pastures, green with grass,
And hear the lowing cattle's call,
To see the swallows in their flight,
I know God made them one and all.
To some, the house may seem secure,
May fill their needs from strength within;
But oh, for me, to gaze outside
Gives me such joy and hope of men!

Mary S. Chevalier

Autumn's Mirrored Everywhere

Autumn is in the valley,
It dews the grass each morn;
It strolls among the meadows
And pastures, cattle-worn.
It skims across the corn fields
Where ripened cobs hang low;
It's seen in frost that sparkles
On pumpkins' ripe orange glow.
Autumn is on the hillsides;
It's midst the forests, too.
It's mirrored in the sunsets
And in the harvest moon.
Autumn in all its beauty
Just everywhere abounds
And if we look still closer,
Too, in our hearts it's found.

Loise Pinkerton Fritz

*The earth is the Lord's
and the fullness thereof.*
Psalm 24:1

29

Golden Gifts

The trees sway softly in the breeze
Against a sky so blue,
The golden sun beams in across
A sea of morning dew.

My spirit quickens as I see
How much God really cares
To create such beauty just for me;
Reaching out, I take my share.

If man isn't willing to take the time,
How can he truly live,
If he looks at neither sky nor sun,
Which God so freely gives?

I wish that I could save this day
And the radiance that I view,
But I will hold in memory
Its gifts of gold and blue.

Sara I. Brown

Point of View

Thank You for Your beauty, Lord.
At times I don't look out.
I only look within and see
My shades of pain and doubt.
But if I looked at You, Lord,
Amidst Your clouds on high,
My worries would become as clouds
And softly drift on by.

Margaret Peterson

31

These Prayers We Offer

Dear God, where there is darkness,
We pray there will be light.
Wherever there's injustice,
May justice be in sight.

Where there is great oppression,
May freedom soon be near.
We pray for understanding
And, too, the end of fear.

Where there is utter hopelessness,
May hope be born anew.
May we show more compassion
As You would have us do.

Where there is strife and hatred,
May there be peace and love.
These prayers we humbly offer
To You, dear God above.

Harold F. Mohn

Time Alone

Deep in the silence of the forest
Was where I'd go to be
That I might hear in Nature's stillness
God's voice speak to me.
His voice, it echoed through the trees
When the wind caressed their limbs,
Like angels softly whispering
A thousand prayerful hymns.
And through the brook, His voice, it laughed
A strong and joyful song
Which spoke of His enduring love
As it winded its way along.
He spoke through the clamor of the squirrels
And the owl's solemn cries,
And evening played His symphonies
In the crickets' lullabies.
These melodies, they stirred my soul
To depths no words could express.
Alone in the forest my heart did find
Its greatest happiness.

Victoria Ann Turner

Thank You, God

Every morning that I wake up
With God's glory all around,
I think of all my children
And the happiness I've found.

God sure knew what wealth He brought me
When He put you in my care.
Troubles never stay long with me
'Cause I know you kids are there.

I think of you each morning
With a heart that's full of love,
Hoping God will keep you happy
As He looks down from above.

Hoping that He'll keep you always
In the shelter of His hand
With health and joy abounding
As you live here in His land.

Every day I look toward Heaven
With thanks to God within my heart
'Cause He gave me all you children
And the joys you all impart.

Mabel E. Evans

*And say, "Save us, O God, our Savior,
gather us and deliver us from the nations,
that we may give thanks to Your holy name
and glory in praising You."*
1 Chronicles 16:35

35

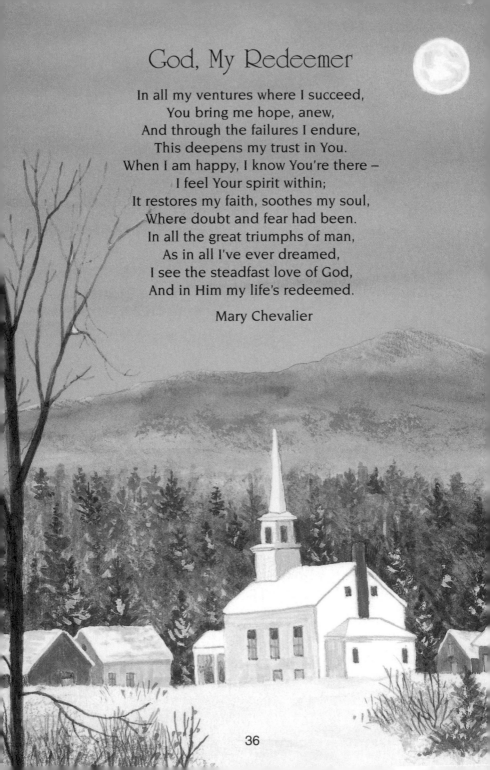

God, My Redeemer

In all my ventures where I succeed,
You bring me hope, anew,
And through the failures I endure,
This deepens my trust in You.
When I am happy, I know You're there –
I feel Your spirit within;
It restores my faith, soothes my soul,
Where doubt and fear had been.
In all the great triumphs of man,
As in all I've ever dreamed,
I see the steadfast love of God,
And in Him my life's redeemed.

Mary Chevalier

In Evening's Peace

Blue twilight soft as angels' wings
Has swept old Winter's sky,
Where icy winds slipped through the trees
And sought the mountains high.
From one small home, one shining light
Illuminates the snow,
Where burns the warmth of love and fire,
As evening's shadows grow.
The smoke ascends the silvered sky,
A pure and silent prayer
That begs the holy grace of God
On all assembled there.
And peace, sweet peace – oh, blessed peace –
It's you that here we find,
Upon the land, upon the house,
Upon the heart and mind!

Kate Watkins Furman

May He grant you joy of
heart and may peace
abide among you.
Sirach 50:23

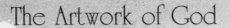

The Artwork of God

In God's aesthetic beauty,
We feel His presence there,
Amidst the fields of burnished grain
And flowers blooming fair.

We see Him in the splendor of
A rainbow 'cross the sky
And in the hue of reddish gold
When evening's drawing nigh.

We feel the mighty hand of God
In every child's embrace;
It's though He may be standing there –
That we are face to face.

We hear God in the quiet sounds
Of waterfalls and rain,
In trilling songs of chickadees,
The bluebird's sweet refrain.

Oh, what is man that God has placed
His artwork to behold?
'Tis here to warm the heart of Him –
And make His story told.

Mary S. Chevalier

Offer Up a Prayer

Did you wake today feeling well?
Did you seem to be free of care?
That was our Father lifting you –
Offer up a prayer.
Did all your burdens seem light?
Was each one easy to bear?
That was our Father carrying you –
Offer up a prayer.
Were you surrounded by loved ones?
Was there happiness to share?
That was our Father touching you –
Offer up a prayer.
As you lay your head on your pillow
Could you feel God's presence there?
He never left you once today –
Offer up a prayer.

Eleanor Torchia

Old Friends

Old friends are not forgotten
Whenever they depart.
They occupy a special place
Deep within the heart.

Years and years of memories
Don't quickly fade away.
The dreams you shared together
Aren't lost in yesterday.

The pain of separation
May linger for a night,
But joy comes in the morning
When everything is bright.

Old friends are not forgotten
When new friends come along.
There's always room for someone new
To help you sing your song.

Clay Harrison

*Bless the Lord, my soul; do
not forget all the gifts of God.*
Psalm 103:2

Winter Can
Be a Lonely Time

Winter can be a lonely time
As the snow and bitter cold
Confine us to the homeplace
And put our dreams on hold.
Stark, barren trees and empty nests
Paint pictures of despair
With no color in the landscape,
No birdsong in the air.
Gray skies add a somber touch
To the woodlands below
Where melancholy shadows
Form ink blots on the snow.

Then suddenly some deer appear
And rabbits come out to play,
And the neighbors come to visit
In one-horse open sleighs.
It doesn't seem so lonely now
With friends and family there,
For Winter can make memories
As warm as springtime air.

Clay Harrison

His Spirit Renews

When we pray to the Father in spirit and mind,
He is faithful to answer our pleas…
But only according to His perfect will,
For He knows the depths of our needs.

When we ask for assistance to guide us through life,
He is there to give shelter and care…
For our great provider and Lord of our lives
Knows how much we love Him through prayer.

We bond with our Father and praise Him each day
When we open our hearts to His truths…
Allowing His presence to fill us with peace,
His spirit so softly renews.

Jill Lemming

*A clean heart create for me, God;
renew in me a steadfast spirit.*
Psalm 51:12

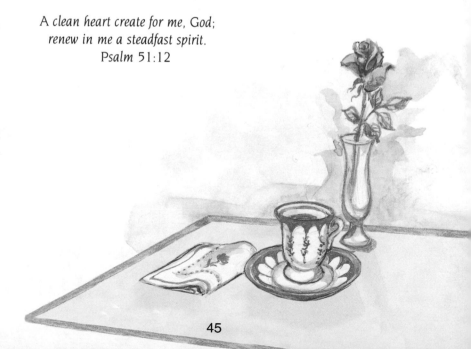

Strolling Life's Garden

While strolling in life's garden,
I saw beauty on every turn;
Bright flowers were all blooming,
Midst stately rows of fern.
Amongst such lovely splendor
Were roses full of thorns.
White lilies aged with browning,
A product of life's storms.
We, too, have thorns and thistles
That prick and cause us pain;
Sometimes we trip and stumble,
But God picks us up again.

Then as we stroll life's garden,
There are signs along the way;
If we will read and follow them,
We won't get lost or stray.
Christ is the garden keeper,
Who tends our needs as well.
As long as we look up to Him,
His love won't let us fail.

Frances Culp Wolfe

Season of Spring

Springtime seems to fill the air
With music all its own;
Frogs and crickets come to life
With such a pleasant tone.
Flowers peek their tiny heads
Above the fertile ground;
No other season of the year
Can such beauty ere be found.
Dear God, I am so thankful
For this season You bestow;
It fills my heart with gladness
And it helps my spirit grow.

Albert Theel

Remembering to Pray

"Ask and it shall be given,"
So the Lord would have you pray,
"Seek and you will surely find,"
For He will show the way.
"Knock and it shall be opened."
Do you think God is about
To turn His back upon you,
Knowing all you are without?
We are as little children
In this valley full of tears;
We need His love to guide us,
Giving meaning through the years.
For to cross life's troubled waters,
There is no better way,
Than clinging tightly to His arm
...And remembering to pray!

Grace E. Easley

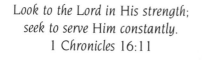

Look to the Lord in His strength;
seek to serve Him constantly.
1 Chronicles 16:11

49

So Many Things to Love

There are so many things to love
Within this world so grand,
From gentle earth to skies above,
Each lovely spot of land;
A friend who wears a happy smile
And lends a fond hello,
The million moments quite worthwhile
And neighbors dear to know.
So many things to call our own –
Each precious springtime day,
The quiet moments spent alone,
A little child at play…

The chance to hold a baby near,
To sing a lullaby,
A happy heart that's free from fear,
A hilltop reaching high;
A whispered prayer, a courage true,
The dreams we dare to dream,
A summer day 'neath skies of blue,
A gentle flowing stream;
The Autumn colors – red and gold –
A faith in God above,
The springtime warmth, the Winter cold…
So many things to love.

Garnett Ann Schultz

Expressions of God's Love

Because God loves you,
Rain comes in the Spring,
Flowers bloom in vibrant hues,
Birds have a song to sing.
Because God loves you,
Winter snow is white,
Trees are forever green,
Stars shine every night!
The universe was created
By God's mighty hand.
Every prayer is answered
By His will and plan.
The reason why the sun shines,
Why the sky above is blue,
Why faith makes all things possible…
Is because of God's love for you!

Millie Torzilli

God's Gifts

Have you ever really thought about
The beauty Nature brings?
Have you listened at the break of day
To a baby robin sing?
Have you seen a pink cloud slipping
Behind an orange sun
When a patch of gray and purple sky
Signal the day is done?
Can you ever walk along a beach
As your toes push through the sand
And not wonder how each grain was formed
In this ever-mighty land?
Do you feel the wonder of it all
With the treasures that you hold?
God's gifts are much more priceless
Than a storehouse full of gold.
Go ahead and count your blessings –
They were yours right from the start.
God's gifts are very precious,
So keep them in your heart.

Penelope Gamble

*One thing I ask of the Lord; this I
seek: To dwell in the Lord's house all
the days of my life, to gaze on the
Lord's beauty, to visit His temple.*
Psalm 27:4

The Journey Home

Don't worry about anything,
For don't you know it's true –
A loving God has launched the ship
That gently carries you!

Each boat that sails the sea of life,
That rocks with every storm,
Is guided through the straits of faith
To a harbor safe and warm.

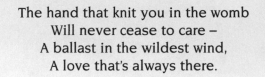

The hand that knit you in the womb
Will never cease to care –
A ballast in the wildest wind,
A love that's always there.

And each man hears a special call
That beckons him alone,
While God provides along the way
The stars that guide him home!

Kate Watkins Furman

A Special Bond

I miss you more than you will know –
Your voice and your bright smile –
And though we must be separated,
It's measured in mere miles…
For our spirits formed a special bond,
So many years ago.
I felt it start that day we met
And time has helped it grow.
No one on earth could take your place;
You've come to mean that much.
We've shared our hearts and Jesus' love
Through you, I've felt His touch.
So come what may in this old world,
From now until the end –
I know for certain we'll remain
The very best of friends.

Denise A. DeWald

Sacred Is the Morning

So sacred is the morning
When I wake to hear the sound
Of the Holy Spirit's "whispers,"
As His peace in me abounds.

The joy comes in the morning
As the Scripture states so true…
And the weeping now is over,
For the night has ended, too.

Oh, thank You, God, my Father,
For You've heard my simple prayer…
To renew Your strength within me
And find comfort in Your care.

Jill Lemming

They that hope in the Lord will renew
their strength, they will soar as with
eagles' wings; They will run and not
grow weary, walk and not grow faint.
Isaiah 40:31

His Wonders

He clothes the world with beauty,
With flowers, grass and trees,
Mountains that stand in majesty
Look down on rolling seas.
Blue skies above, a canvas
For sunset's flaming hues,
Proclaim a wondrous God
Whose love is ever true.

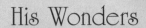

His word to guide our living
That leads us all life long
Brings peace to troubled hearts
And on our lips a song.
We feast upon His miracles
And beauty unsurpassed,
A preview of what is to come
When we reach home at last.
His wonders speak of Heaven,
Worth more than earthly fame,
To share when days on earth are done
For all who love His name.

Helen Gleason

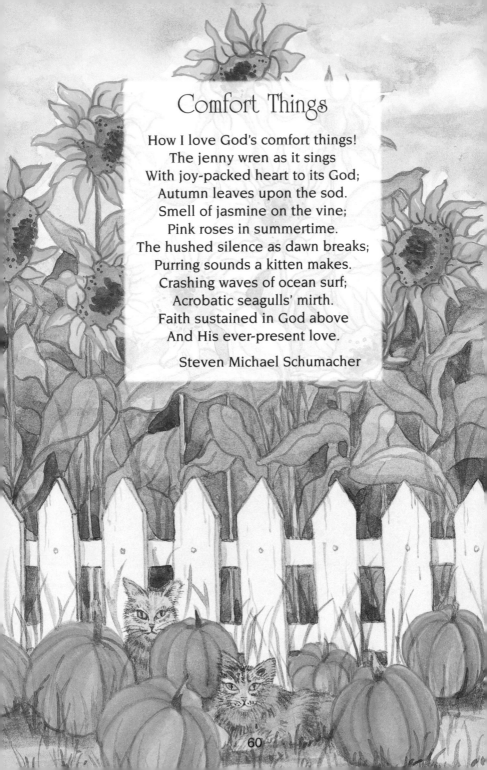

Comfort Things

How I love God's comfort things!
The jenny wren as it sings
With joy-packed heart to its God;
Autumn leaves upon the sod.
Smell of jasmine on the vine;
Pink roses in summertime.
The hushed silence as dawn breaks;
Purring sounds a kitten makes.
Crashing waves of ocean surf;
Acrobatic seagulls' mirth.
Faith sustained in God above
And His ever-present love.

Steven Michael Schumacher

Pretty Autumn

Summer soon will take vacation
Replaced by Autumn's lovely leaves,
All in such pretty colors,
To the eye is sure to please.

Misty morning's golden sunrise
All in wonder of the day,
Pretty Autumn, show your colors –
How I wish that you could stay.

Still we know the Master Painter
Has another wonder plan,
Soon to paint the hills and valleys
Pure and white across the land.

Soon to fall, oh pretty snowflakes,
Spread your blanket of pure white,
Shining, shining like a diamond
By the moon's own golden light.

Katherine Smith Matheney

But the plan of the Lord
stands forever, wise designs
through all generations.
Psalm 33:11

61

A New Day

A new day has sprung;
It's like a new song
That echoes across the land,
With bird song so sweet,
The buzz of the bees…
While God holds this day in His hands.

A new day's begun
With rain or with sun;
Matters not what it may be.
The rain brings the flowers,
The sun dries the showers;
Awake! Now God's beauties see.

A new day is here,
Oh, greet it with cheer;
It ne'er will return again.
Give thanks for this day,
Then live it God's way,
Praising His holy name.

Loise Pinkerton Fritz

*That I may praise God's
name in song and glorify it
with thanksgiving.*
Psalm 69:31

Thank You, Lord

Thank You, Lord, for loving us
No matter what our ways.
Thank You, Lord, for staying near
Until our end of days.
Thank You, Lord, for answering us
Each moment that we call.
Thank You, Lord, for giving us
Gifts both great and small.
Thank You, Lord, for keeping us
Safe from every harm,
And thank You, Lord, for holding us
So gently in Your arms.

Eva Marie Ippolito

A Little Tender Care

Just a little tender care
And the sweetest rose will grow.
Just a little tender care
And God will make it so.
Just a little tender care
And the baby bird will fly.
Just a little tender care
Then he will own the sky.
Just a little tender care
And our loved ones will know
That they are truly blessed,
For love has made it so.
All the things we say and do
And all the things we share
Can make this place like God intends
With just a little tender care.

Chet Stanhope

This Is the Day

This is the day that the Lord has made –
I will rejoice and be glad in it.
I will start out this day with a song in my heart
To face any trial and to win it…
For I know that I walk with His hand in mine,
He will guide every step of my way.
If I fail or I fall, He will lift me up,
The Lord is my strength everyday.
This is the day that I will be glad –
I can smile, I can win and achieve.
For I've given my heart to my God this day
And I trust in His word – I believe.

I believe that He has a plan for me,
That my life will be changed for the best.
He has washed all my sins, He has made me whole.
I'm at peace, I am calm – I am blessed.
This is the day that I overcome
All the burdens that weigh on my heart.
My spirit will soar and I will succeed,
For I'm given a fresh new start.
I will walk with pride with my head held high,
And fear cannot enter my sphere.
For this is the day that the Lord has made –
All is well, all is good… God is near.

Patience Allison Hartbauer

Where We Are... God Is

We do not need cathedral's spire
Or stone-carved temple grand.
To worship our dear God above –
We can pray just where we stand.

We do not need the songs of choirs,
Though beautiful they are.
We can sing our own sweet praises
As we travel near and far.

We can stand in fields of new grain,
On the desert, shore or glen,
Make our vow of sweet surrender
And begin our lives again.

With renewed life, love and spirit,
Casting off our worldly care,
We can face each awesome challenge
Knowing God is always there.

Gertrude Blau Byram

A Listening Heart

Dear Lord, I want a listening heart,
Not only ears that hear,
For only when I listen well
Your presence feels so near.
I want my eyes to see much more,
Not just a small, small part,
For eyes may not reveal as much
Seen by a loving heart.
My lips may speak so many words,
But they may be in vain;
The listening heart is open to
Another's grief and pain.
There's so much pain and sorrow, Lord;
I need to feel You near.
Just give me words and eyes that see
And, Lord, a heart that hears.
I thank You for Your loving care
And Lord I humbly pray
For love enough to pass along
To those along life's way.
Perhaps they need some "comfort" words,
But that is only part —
So in the quiet of the hour
I want a listening heart.

Gertrude B. McClain

Positive Faith

My Lord and my God,
My one and my all,
By faith hold me up
If perhaps I should fall.

When in the dark valleys
Of deep misery and despair,
Please give me true faith
To know You are there.

Faith can move mountains;
It's God's holy word.
We can reach life's peaks
By His message we've heard.

God is the essence and core
Of my positive faith alone.
On earth He'll walk with me
Until He calls me safely home.

Shirley Hile Powell

Simple Trust

Have you ever wondered how
Trees come alive in Spring…
Barren branches fill with leaves
With new buds opening?
And have you seen the crocus
Push right up through the snow?
How could it know the timing
Was right for it to show?
The lily bulb, long dormant,
In frozen, icy ground
Awakens from its slumber,
Spreads beauty all around.
Knowing leaves that drop in Fall
Appear again in Spring…
Shouldn't it be simple to
Trust God for everything?

Anna M. Matthews

Autumn's in the Air

Autumn's glorious dwindling days
Mirror sunset's scarlet rays.
Butterflies flit by in grace,
Hurrying to their hiding place.
The evening air now holds a chill
As Fall, her vibrant colors spill.
Yesterday summertime was king
But Fall today is in full swing.
The harvest moon, a lantern bright,
Showers the stars with brilliant light.
As I gaze at the heavens and say a prayer,
I thank the Lord for His autumn-wear.

Nora M. Bozeman

*I have heard that the spirit of God
is in you, that you possess
brilliant knowledge and
extraordinary wisdom.*
Daniel 5:14

Friendship

As I sit by the willows,
Lost in deep thought,
Dear memories of you surface
With all that you've brought
To the friendship we've cherished
Throughout passing years,
Bringing joy and sweet laughter –
And just a few tears.
Remember the springtimes,
The Summers and Fall,
The Winters and sleigh times?
How we savored them all!

The seasons have lengthened
And we've gone separate ways,
But I've never forgotten
Those blest, happy days.
And though space now divides us,
And keeps us apart,
I hardly need tell you
You're close in my heart.
For I'll always remember
With gratitude-plus
The importance of friendships,
Dear memories of us.

Vi B. Chevalier

Behold Thy Children

Behold Thy children, precious Lord,
In all parts of the earth –
Uplift each heart and guide each mind,
And give each child its birth…
Behold Thy children, precious Lord,
Of every clime and creed –
Fulfill their many dreams, oh Lord,
And sanctify each need…
Behold Thy children, precious Lord,
Of every tongue and race,
And put salvation in each soul,
And a smile on every face!

Hope C. Oberhelman

Forever Friend

Sometimes I get to thinking
Of the friendship that we share
And my heart is filled with gladness,
Just to know that you're there.
For you have a way about you
That is honest and sincere,
A happiness that radiates
And makes you very dear.
You have the art of making
The shadows fade away;
You bring an extra sparkle
To an ordinary day.
I never knew how down I was
Until you came along;
You changed my tune of sadness
Into a happy song.
A cross is not so heavy
When it is borne by two;
Life's road is not so weary,
When I'm walking it with you.
Of all the gifts God has bestowed
And been disposed to send,
Not one of them could ever mean
As much as you, my friend.

Grace E. Easley

The Seasons Onward Flow

The seasons come, the seasons go,
And in between the hours flow,
Bringing springtime's floral blooms
Wafting forth a sweet perfume.

The seasons come, the seasons go,
And in between the days all flow,
Bringing joys of summertime
And serenity sublime.

The seasons come, the seasons go,
And in between the weeks all flow,
Bringing us the harvest moon
And the earth with bounty strewn.

The seasons come, the seasons go,
And in between the months all flow,
Bringing snowflakes falling down
On the Winter's frozen ground.

The seasons come, the seasons go;
Through them all, God's love still flows.

Loise Pinkerton Fritz

But I will not take my love
from Him, nor will I betray
my bond of loyalty.
Psalm 89:34

Little Acts of Kindness

Little acts of kindness may
Chase somebody's blues away.
A smile, a look, a fond "hello"
Is a gift that you can bestow.
When a soul is in distress
And they send an SOS,
A smile can go a long, long way
When a life has gone astray.
Don't be afraid to say, "hello"
Or help someone who's feeling low,
For smiles will lift one's spirit up
And happiness will fill his cup.
Little acts of kindness bring
A happiness awakening,
So with a smile and friendly nod,
Give the gift that comes from God.

Nora M. Bozeman

Rebirth

Like nimble rabbits on the run,
The leaves of Autumn, one by one,
Scatter 'cross the lawn and street
In carefree chase, on dancing feet.
Free at last to roam and play,
Free to fly whichever way,
And then, as Winter winds blow cold,
To cling together and to hold
Warm visions of a joyous Spring
When life renews and everything
Holds promise of a Summer bright
With sweet rebirth in blest sunlight.
Though seasons come and seasons go,
Life shall go on – God made it so.

VI B. Chevalier

The Lord, your God, is in your midst, a
mighty Savior; He will rejoice over you
with gladness, and renew you in His love,
He will sing joyfully because of you.
Zephaniah 3:17

81

Evening Peace

Night winds in the lofty pines
Sing a soft lullaby.
The sun has settled in the west;
First stars adorn the sky.

'Round about dark shadows grow,
Birds have hushed their songs;
Now only to the restless wind
The tranquil earth belongs.

Angels with their wings unfurled
Guard the slumbering land,
And every weary soul finds rest
In God's almighty hand.

Regina Wiencek

A Different Way to View the Day

In the race to get things done
We struggle to stay afloat;
Each task is an overwhelming obstacle,
Each sound, a discordant note.
Our peace and joy get misplaced;
We tend to neglect our Friend.
Look up and see! God's sun shines still;
We're headed to life without end.
Ask the Lord for wisdom;
Let Him set the priority.
Each day can be less stressful
When we let Him set us free.

Elaine Hardt

He set me free in the open; He
rescued me because He loves me.
Psalm 18:20

By His Strength

God has given us the wings
To fly across this land,
Bearing witness to His word
And offering His hand.

Bringing faith to those who mourn
And comforting the weak,
Giving glory to the One
Whose gentle touch we seek.

Building bridges to His love
That others will not cry.
God has given us the wings
And by His strength we'll fly.

Jill Lemming

My strength and my courage is
the Lord, and He has been my Savior.
He is my God, I praise Him; the God
of my Father, I extol Him.
Exodus 15:2

Just a Simple Prayer

Sometimes just a simple prayer
Can make a big difference in your life;
It can spark some hope, inner peace,
Through all the trials and strife.
A prayer that's whispered sincerely
From the heart on bended knee
Can paint such a colorful rainbow
While the stormy clouds begin to flee.
Prayer can move a mountain
If we trust that God knows best.
Perhaps instead He'll give us strength
To climb and meet the test.

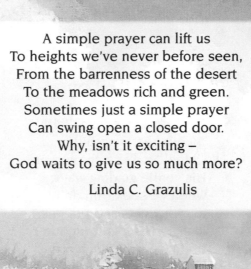

A simple prayer can lift us
To heights we've never before seen,
From the barrenness of the desert
To the meadows rich and green.
Sometimes just a simple prayer
Can swing open a closed door.
Why, isn't it exciting –
God waits to give us so much more?

Linda C. Grazulis

Share His Love

When we carry enough faith
In our hearts each day,
We'll feel God's saving power,
His gentle guiding ways.
When we seek Him daily
In our thoughts and prayers,
We'll share His love with others
Upon life's thoroughfare.
By kindly thoughts and deeds,
His will is being done,
For the Father loves us all,
Each and every one.

Jacqui Richardson

Our hope for you is firm,
for we know that as you share in
the sufferings, you also share
in the encouragement.
2 Corinthians 1:7

In Just a While

In just a while the clouds will disappear,
Once more I'll see a rainbow in the sky.
Though now this world of mine is colored gray,
The sun will shine upon me by and by.
My heart is heavy with a nameless grief
That seems to almost take my breath away,
But in a while I know that peace will come,
And pain will leave and only joy will stay.
In just a while all I am feeling now
Will disappear as if it never was,
And I will breathe a sigh of pure relief
To find that I can smile again because...
Nothing lasts forever in this world,
God only sends the crosses we can bear,
And sorrow fades before my firm belief
That God walks close beside me everywhere!

Grace E. Easley

*Your love is before my
eyes; I walk guided by
Your faithfulness.
Psalm 26:3*

89

Thanksgiving

Let us thank our Lord today
For the sun that shines in May,
For the budding cherry trees,
The greening of the country leaves.

Let us thank our Lord today
For Summer's lovely golden stay,
The daisies wild in meadows green,
The garden squash and climbing bean.

Let us thank our Lord today
For Autumn's beauty in its stay,
The sumac red and scarlet elm,
Nature in its vibrant realm.

Let us thank our Lord today
For Winter's beauty at our bay,
The warmth of home at fireside,
The crystal scenes of acres wide.

Let us thank our Lord today
For every season's special way,
And know that we are truly blessed,
From north to south and east to west.

Virginia Borman Grimmer

Hold Me, Jesus

Hold me, Jesus, when I'm sad
And things are, oh, so wrong;
Help me see beyond the hurt –
Place in my heart a song.

Hold me, Jesus, when I cry
And see the world through tears;
Comfort me with whispered words
That drive away my fears.

Hold me, Jesus, let me feel
The wonder of Thy love;
As I lift my eyes to Thee,
Send peace from up above.

And when at last my heart is still,
Your loving arms around me,
Let me look upon Thy face
And see Thy wondrous glory!

Denise A. DeWald

*If I fly with the wings of dawn and alight
beyond the sea, even there Your hand will
guide me, Your right hand hold me fast.*
Psalm 139:9-10

Sunset Years

Time becomes more precious
As seasons come and go.
Each dawning day's a special gift
When twilight shadows grow.
And looking back I see God's hand
In happiness and sorrow.
He has a purpose for my life,
A plan for each tomorrow.
Faithfully, He brought me through
The valleys in my life.
He took my heart and molded it
Through pain and grief and strife.
He met me on the mountaintop
To catch a fleeting view
Of love and joy unspeakable,
That thrilled me through and through.
Throughout life's changing seasons,
I found God ever near.
Into the sunset of my years,
I walk without a fear.

Regina Wiencek

Thanks be to God for
His indescribable gift!
2 Corinthians 9:15

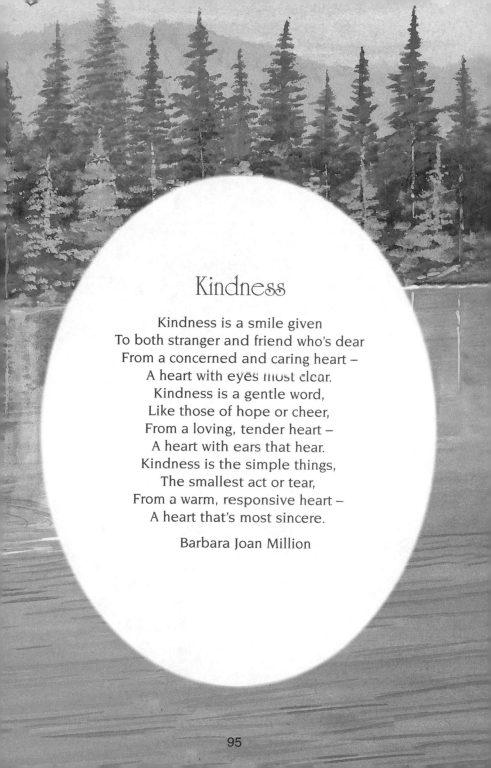

Kindness

Kindness is a smile given
To both stranger and friend who's dear
From a concerned and caring heart –
A heart with eyes most clear.
Kindness is a gentle word,
Like those of hope or cheer,
From a loving, tender heart –
A heart with ears that hear.
Kindness is the simple things,
The smallest act or tear,
From a warm, responsive heart –
A heart that's most sincere.

Barbara Joan Million

Live for Today

Yesterday's a memory,
Tomorrow's just a hope,
Today is our reality
As through life's trials we cope.

But we can live in victory
Relying solely on the Lord.
Commit each day to Him
And peace will be your reward.

The past is gone forever,
The future's a dream away,
But we can live each day that comes
In victory, if we pray.

Remember to give thanks each day
And He'll be by our side,
Then each day will be happy
With Jesus as our guide.

Helen Gleason

*If possible, on your part,
live at peace with all.*
Romans 12:18

Cleansing Rain

Wash away my troubles,
Wash away my pain,
Let me come to You, Lord,
While walking in the rain.
Yes, I'm thinking hardships,
There's discord in my home;
So many of my problems
Follow where'er I roam.

I reach to You for blessings,
I look to You for light;
I need the hope of You, Lord,
To help me make things right.
I ask You for Your spirit,
I need to feel refreshed,
So let the rain revive my soul…
I'm sad, You may have guessed.
It's raining harder now, Lord,
The problems may remain,
But now I'm feeling stronger
While walking in the rain.

Janice Cortis Kasowski

God Is the Light

Amid the turmoil in this world
And all the problems that exist,
Always be aware that God
Is forever in our midst.
He is the shining beacon;
He is the guiding light;
The hope that is enduring
Through every day and night.
For when we stay within His light,
He will guide us as we sail
Through tempest storms confronting us;
God's the light that will not fail.
He will lead us to safe harbor,
Keeping vigil as we go.
No harm can ever come to us
When we stay within God's glow.

Patience Allison Hartbauer

God saw how good the light
was. God then separated the
light from the darkness.
Genesis 1:4

Laugh at the Clouds

Laugh at the clouds
As they sail slowly by.
Smile at the sunshine
In the bright azure sky.

Sway with the hollyhocks
And dance in the breeze.
Sing sweet melodies
With the songbirds in trees.

Enjoy the graceful flight
Of our fine-feathered friends
As they soar high and swiftly
Under the rainbow's bend.

Enjoy the starlit night
And full moon's glow.
Listen to the music
Of the swift river's flow.

Gather in God's beauty
That He made for us with care,
And always be thankful
As you go to Him in prayer.

Shirley Hile Powell

Little Deeds

Little deeds of kindness,
Little acts of love,
Show that we're acquainted
With the Lord above.
Little deeds of kindness
Cheer us on our way,
And help ourselves and others
Have a happy day.
Acts of loving kindness
Prompt a happy smile,
And add a joy to living
And make life worthwhile.

Vera Beall Parker

A Little Prayer

When I awoke this morning
I said a little prayer,
And so I send this message
To let you know I care...
When you are feeling blue
And you think you are alone,
Just remember God is with you
Wherever you may roam...
And He will keep you in His arms
Of comfort and of rest.
His love will be sufficient –
He'll give you what is best.
So, friend, don't be discouraged,
For you are in His care.
Just come into His presence
And God will meet you there.

Bonnie R. Benedix

*I say to the Lord: You are
my God; listen, Lord,
to the words of my prayer.*
Psalm 140:7

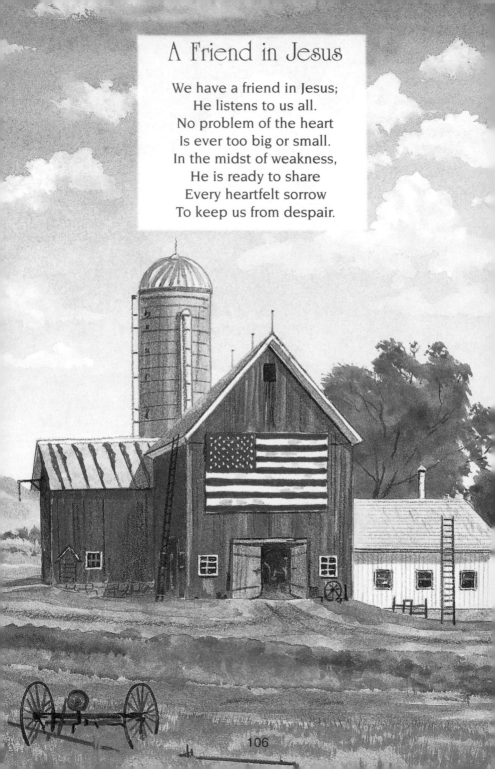

A Friend in Jesus

We have a friend in Jesus;
He listens to us all.
No problem of the heart
Is ever too big or small.
In the midst of weakness,
He is ready to share
Every heartfelt sorrow
To keep us from despair.

He sees every sadness,
Keeps unwept tears at bay,
Always here to guide us,
See us through each day.
When we leave ourselves
Safely in His care,
We feel His gentle comfort
Upon life's thoroughfare,
Giving us the strength
To rise above our trials,
Face the world with courage
And a willing smile,
Knowing in our hearts
We only need to pray,
And He will help us overcome
Whatever comes our way.

Jacqui Richardson

Just Believe

God cares for you each moment,
Each minute and each hour,
Through days of laughter in the sun,
Through dark days filled with showers.
He listens to each prayer that's prayed
And answers with what's best,
Not always what we ask for,
But far better are we blessed.
His love knows no known measure,
No bounds nor depths too deep,
It knows not of conditions –
A promise our God keeps.
How very blessed we are indeed
For One, such as He,
That gives so much and in return
Just asks us to believe.

Gina Mazzullo Laurin

Our Lord Is Always There

Our dear Lord is always there
To share our fears and care;
He gladdens up the saddest heart –
We know He's always there.
Beset by problems past our scope
To solve and to repair,
The answers come from Him above –
Our Lord is always there.
And when we find that troubles seem
Too difficult to bear,
He always lightens up the load –
Our Lord is always there.
He shares our fears, our hopes and dreams
With love beyond compare,
And makes our lives more beautiful,
For He is always there.

Dolores Karides

*And all who heard Him were
astounded at His understanding
and His answers.*
Luke 2:47

O Precious Father

O precious Father, give me time
To meditate on You;
Grant me Godly wisdom
When deciding what to do.
Bless me with serenity
When I seek Your perfect way,
And diligence to walk the path…
That I should never stray.
Keep my heart and eyes affixed
To the life that You proclaim;
Help me accept your chastisement
When I'm the one to blame.

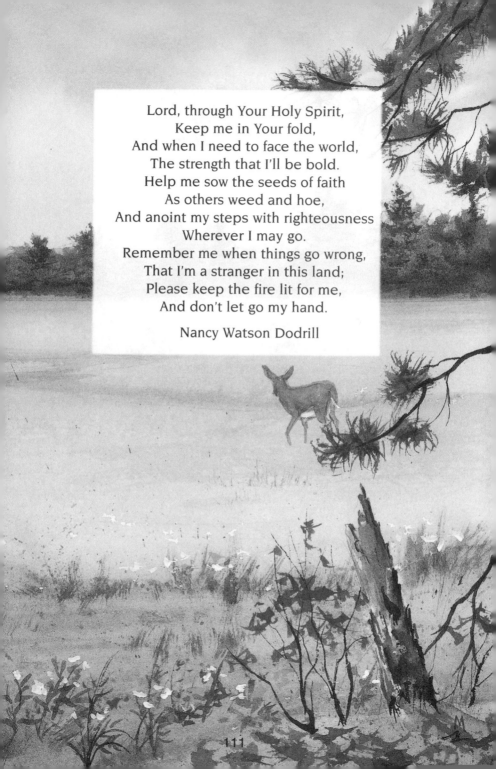

Lord, through Your Holy Spirit,
Keep me in Your fold,
And when I need to face the world,
The strength that I'll be bold.
Help me sow the seeds of faith
As others weed and hoe,
And anoint my steps with righteousness
Wherever I may go.
Remember me when things go wrong,
That I'm a stranger in this land;
Please keep the fire lit for me,
And don't let go my hand.

Nancy Watson Dodrill

Make Life Brighter

Try to make life brighter
In what you do and say.
Bring a smile to someone's face
Each and every day.
Everyone needs some kindness
To lighten up their way,
And in return our loving God
Will truly bless your day.

Nettie Gornick

Whispers

As you drop to your knees to pray today,
As you tell God of your hopes and fears,
Remember each thought and word you say
Is a whisper in God's ear.

Tell Him what concerns you,
Ask Him to calm your fears,
And if you look closely you can see
God smiling through your tears.

Thank Him for your many blessings,
For the special closeness you share!
Open your heart and receive His love,
And know it's always there.

This time of prayer is special –
Sharing words only He can hear.
Because each thought and word you say
Is a whisper in God's ear.

Jane W. Johnson

*If you and your children are
well and your affairs are going as
you wish, I thank God very much,
for my hopes are in Heaven.*
2 Maccabees 9:20

113

Along Right Paths

Lord, let me hear You whisper
And recognize Your voice,
For I am at the crossroads
And need to make a choice.
There are so many pathways,
But only one is right.
Point me in Your way, Lord.
I'll let You be my light.
Allow the path to shine
And illuminate with You,
As Your presence goes before me

And shows me what to do.
May each step I take be grounded
In the knowledge that You care,
And that I can have confidence
Because You're always there.
No road is too long or hard
When it's You who leads the way.
I'll follow Your footsteps, Lord,
On the path I walk this day.

Nancy Janiga

Happy the people who know You, Lord,
who walk in the radiance of Your face.
Psalm 89:16

Winter's Splendor

Glorious sunshine,
Glistening snow;
Blue skies above,
The white earth below.
Pathless wide fields
In stillness abound;
No footprints mar
The snow-covered ground.
Beckoning me
To come out and see
The wondrous beauty
God created for me.
Leaving all cares
And worries behind,
Finding new joy
And sweet peace of mind.

Regina Wiencek

Always Look Ahead

When I look back on years gone by,
I see the error of my ways.
But let me not build monuments
To senseless, empty, Godless days.
By looking back, I waste today
And add to my own sorrow.
While sifting through my deep regrets,
I'll also miss tomorrow.
So, let me use the lessons learned
That old mistakes are not to dread.
They're but a stepping stone to teach us
That we should always look ahead.
The God who gave me past and present,
In Holy Scriptures has He said,
That He will guide my every footstep
If I but trust and look ahead.

Shirley Takacs

*Guide me in Your truth and teach me, for
You are God my savior. For You I wait all the
long day, because of Your goodness, Lord.*
Psalm 25:5

Thank You, God

I thank You, God, for loving me
In spite of wrongs I do.
You always have been there for me
When I have called on You.

I count my blessings one by one
And see Your kindness there,
Though I ofttimes fail to thank You
Midst rush of daily care.

Help me, dear God, to measure up
Whatever is life's test,
To always strive to do what's right
And give to You my best.

Within my heart it's my desire
To walk with You each day,
To know Your dear companionship
Each step along the way.

For bleak and dark would be me life
Without Your love and grace.
And, oh, the joy to know someday
I'll see You face to face.

Kay Hoffman

Find your delight in the Lord who will
give you your heart's desire.
Psalm 37:4

In the Midst of Darkness

In the midst of darkness,
Loneliness and sorrow,
The Lord has made a promise
For a brighter tomorrow.
He assures me in His word that things
Happen for a reason,
And although it's hard to comprehend,
It is only for a season.
For, like Winter when it vanishes
And springtime takes its place,
Sorrow also dissipates
When joy comes by grace.
And the smile that seems to only
Be a memory to you
Will soon be back upon your face
And laughter with it, too.
So rest assured that Jesus keeps
His promises to us,
If we believe and pray to Him
And never cease to trust.

Beverly Huff

Do You Wonder?

Have you ever stopped to wonder
As you gazed up in the sky –
What keeps the stars from falling,
What makes the clouds roll by?
What makes the moon replace the sun
And night replace the day?
What brings sweet peace when day is done
As you homeward went your way?
Have you ever stopped to wonder
How from a tiny seed
Springs forth a fragrant flower
With beauty rare indeed?
What brings the leaves back on the trees
After a Winter of ice and snow?
Do you wonder about such things,
Or skip it and let it go?
So stop and think from day to day
As on through life you trod,
Of the many blessings sent your way
Through the mighty hand of God.

Vernice D. Smith

Be My Master Today

Lord, be my Master today
And go with me where'er I go;
Guard my lips each word I say
And let my light to others show.
Lord, be my Master today
And let Thy will be mine,
For You know what is best for me
And the hills that I must climb.
You know the burdens that I must bear
And the joys to come my way,
So give me the wisdom to accept it all
And be my Master today.

Lord, be my Master today
And let me be Your child;
Send Your angels to encircle me
As I travel each weary mile.
So let me follow You, Lord,
And not go any faster
Than Your footsteps will lead me...
Today, Lord, be my Master.

Hazel Yoho

*You are my rock and my
fortress; for Your name's sake
lead and guide me.*
Psalm 31:4

The Silent Days of Winter

The silent days of Winter wear
Snowbound skies and ermine hair,
Icicles and crispy morns,
Snowflakes that are heaven-born.
Coats and gloves are now a must,
And walking is adventurous.
The silent days of Winter call,
On padded feet my footsteps fall;
Every day brings new delights
In spite of Winter's chilly bites.
So let it snow and let it ice,
For this is God's Winter paradise!

Nora M. Bozeman

His Touch

I see silos in the distance
Among the leaves of red and gold.
I look in awe and wonder
As I see God's touch unfold.

As I travel down life's highway,
I see Him everywhere.
I'm on the road to Heaven
And I see His touch so fair.

The mountains that I've had to climb
Grow straight beneath my feet,
As I look ahead and see Him there,
My Savior, oh so sweet.

Dona M. Maroney

*Hallelujah! How good to celebrate
our God in song; how sweet to
give fitting praise.*
Psalm 147:1

For where your treasure is,
there also will your heart be.
Luke 12:34

Family

A family is a wondrous thing
Bringing joy to hearts;
In trials it can comfort bring
As love it does impart.

A family means belonging
And standing by always.
We know we never are alone
And together we can pray.

Our earthly family is a gift
To be treasured with Your love;
'Tis a vision of the family
We'll share in Heaven above.

Helen Gleason

Winter's Return

Seasons come and seasons go –
Autumn leaves must fall.
The splendor of the earth gives way
To Winter's chilling call.
Birds flock to now-empty fields
And gather in bare trees
To leave the northern shores behind
Before the coming freeze.
The earth grows still, the earth grows cold,
Unyielding, wild winds roam.
Through the lingering twilight haze
Lights shine from every home.
Wood smoke from the chimneys drift
Across the brown terrain,
And suddenly, without a sound,
Snowflakes fall again.

Regina Wiencek